Anonymous

The Buffalo Library and Its Building

Illustrated with views. Also brief historical sketches of the Buffalo fine arts academy, the Buffalo society of natural sciences, and the Buffalo historical society, which occupy parts of the same building

Anonymous

The Buffalo Library and Its Building
Illustrated with views. Also brief historical sketches of the Buffalo fine arts
academy, the Buffalo society of natural sciences, and the Buffalo historical society,
which occupy parts of the same building

ISBN/EAN: 9783337426484

Printed in Europe, USA, Canada, Australia, Japan

Cover: Foto ©ninafisch / pixelio.de

More available books at **www.hansebooks.com**

THE
··BUFFALO · LIBRARY··
AND ITS
···BUILDING···

···ILLUSTRATED · WITH · VIEWS···

LSO · BRIEF · HISTORICAL · SKETCHES · OF · THE
BUFFALO FINE ARTS ACADEMY, · THE
BUFFALO · SOCIETY · OF · NATURAL · SCIENCES,
AND · THE · BUFFALO · HISTORICAL · SOCIETY, · WHICH
OCCUPY · PARTS · OF · THE · SAME · BUILDING.

MDCCCLXXXVII

The Buffalo Library.

THE BUFFALO LIBRARY.

HISTORICAL SKETCH.

THE BUFFALO LIBRARY was known during the first fifty years of its life as the Library of the Young Men's Association, or, in common speech, as the Young Men's Library, of Buffalo. An earlier 'Buffalo Library'— a little village collection of books, about seven hundred in number — had been formed in 1816, by a small company of stockholders who held together until 1832. A second library and literary society was organized near the close of 1830, under the name of the Buffalo Lyceum, which seemed vigorous for a time in several directions of activity, but which had no long existence. It was not until the winter of 1836 that a movement with some really lasting energy in it was set on foot, and resulted in the organization of the Young Men's Association of the city of Buffalo. The incidents and circumstances of that movement were investigated carefully by the late Charles D. Norton, when he prepared his historical address, delivered on the occasion of the celebration of the twenty-fifth anniversary of the Association, in 1861, and he wrote: 'If it were necessary to state the names of the men who deserve the title of founders of this Association, it could only be said that the general and recognized necessity for such an institution induced a variety of effort, in which all the young men of the place were more or less engaged. The letters furnished to me, by gentlemen of this city, render it not a little difficult to determine whose is the especial honor, but they indicate the general interest taken in it by our citizens.' In the *Commercial Advertiser* of February 20, 1836, Mr. Norton found the following notice, signed by nearly four hundred citizens, ' comprising all classes, trades, and professions' :

Y. M. ASSOCIATION.—The young men of Buffalo friendly to the foundation of a Young Men's Association for mutual improvement in literature and science, are requested to meet at the Court House on Monday, the 22d day of February, at the hour of 7 P. M.

At the meeting which followed this notice, Hon. Hiram Pratt presided, and Richard L. Allen and Isaac W. Skinner were secretaries. A constitution had been previously prepared at the office of Mr. Seth C. Hawley, copied in a great degree from that of the Young Men's Association at Albany, which was submitted to this meeting by Mr. Frederick P. Stevens. After some sharp discussion the constitution was adopted, and an adjournment was had to the 29th of the same month, that the constitution might be examined and subscribed. On the adjourned day Mr. Roswell W. Haskins presided, Mr. George E. Hayes was secretary, and a committee of seven was appointed to nominate officers; and, with Mr. Henry K. Smith and Mr. Dyre Tillinghast acting as tellers, the persons who had become members elected as president Seth C. Hawley; Dr. Charles Winne, Samuel N. Callender, and George Brown as vice-presidents; Frederick P. Stevens, corresponding secretary; A. G. C. Cochrane, recording secretary; and John R. Lee, treasurer. The managers chosen were Oliver G. Steele, Henry K. Smith, William H. Lacy, Geo. W. Allen, Chas. H. Raymond, Henry R. Williams, George E. Hayes, Halsey R. Wing, Rushmore Poole, and Hunting S. Chamberlain.

In 1861, Mr. Norton reported all the members of this first board of managers living, except H. K. Smith, William H. Lacy, and Henry R. Williams. At the present writing (March, 1887), the sole survivor of the entire board of original officers is Mr. John R. Lee, its treasurer.

The Association came into existence at a time when everybody felt rich. It was the year of bubbles in land speculation which preceded the great collapse of 1837. A subscription that ran up to $6,700 in amount was raised with astonishing ease to give the new library a solid footing. The books of the old Buffalo Library and of the Lyceum were transferred to it, considerable purchases were made under a contract with the Messrs. Butler, and 2,700 volumes in all were collected before the end of the year. The chief feature of the institution, however, was its newspaper reading-room, where six quarterly, ten monthly and forty-four weekly publications were on file, and which boasted of being the completest in any city west of New-York.

The financial crash of 1837 swept many imagined fortunes out of existence, and with them a great part of the small endowment which the library was supposed to have secured in the subscriptions alluded to above. Its membership fell away, it was weighted with some debt which it had contracted too hopefully, and for half-a-dozen years, or more, it struggled doubtfully and hard between life and death. But there was pluck in the young men of those days, and a Spartan band among them stood fast by the Association through all difficulties until the coming of more prosperous times. Not, however, until 1845, under the presidency of Mr. Gibson T. Williams, was it cleared of debt and fairly launched upon its successful career.

The original rooms of the Association were on the upper floors of the building then owned by Mr. Joseph Dart, numbered 175 Main street, now numbered 219, being three doors below Seneca street. Mr. B. W. Jenks, a portrait painter, occupied adjoining rooms and became nominally the first librarian by reason of that circumstance, undertaking to overlook the library while pursuing his own work. In reality, the functions of the first librarian were performed by Mr. J. F. Young, of Williamsville, then a lad taking lessons in art from Mr. Jenks, and to whom the latter delegated the care of the neighboring books and newspapers. Subsequently, the post was accepted by Dr. Charles H. Raymond, who had been prominent among the founders of the library and foremost in activity of effort to sustain it. The labor that he assumed, said Mr. Norton, speaking in 1861, and the patience he displayed under great discouragements, and the resolution with which he persisted in his unrewarded toil, assign to him a place among its chief benefactors. He was a ripe and good scholar, and had all a scholar's modesty. Dr. Raymond served as librarian until some time in

1839, when he was succeeded by Mr. Phineas Sargeant, who remained at the desk until 1850.

In May, 1841, the Association removed to South Division street, in rooms over the shops now numbered 15 and 16, the library being at one side of the stairway, while a small lecture room was fitted up on the other side. These rooms became inadequate and unsuitable before many years had passed. The first movement which the discontent with them engendered took the form of a building project, and in 1848 the undertaking was very seriously set on foot. It went so far that a building committee, having the matter in charge, bought a lot of ground for the purpose, 48 feet front by 91 feet deep, on the north side of Eagle street, between Main and Pearl streets, for $3,000. This was done, however, on their individual responsibility. They procured plans and specifications, contemplating a structure which would cost from $8,000 to $12,000. They secured the passage of an act authorizing the Association to borrow $15,000 on its bonds, and they invited subscriptions from citizens in aid of the project. An elegant blank-book, richly bound in Russia leather, with an inscription upon the side: 'Building subscriptions, Young Men's Association, 1848,' is still preserved among the archives of the library. But, alas! its inviting white leaves have no stain of ink. Not an autograph is found in it.

The premature building project came to naught; but it had its effect, without doubt, in stimulating a movement to the American Block, which took place in 1852. American Hall was leased, with commodious rooms for the library underneath, and the circumstances as well as the situation of the Association were greatly improved. The hall became a source of considerable income; the annual lecture courses grew more popular and profitable; membership increased and the course of advancing prosperity was generally smoothed.

Meantime, in 1850, failing health had caused the resignation of Mr. Phineas Sargeant from the librarianship and Mr. Lewis Jenkins succeeded to him. But a few months after the removal in 1852 Mr. Jenkins resigned, in his turn, and Mr. William Ives was appointed in his place.

A period of twelve uneventful years followed, during which the Association and its library gained slowly but steadily in strength and character. As

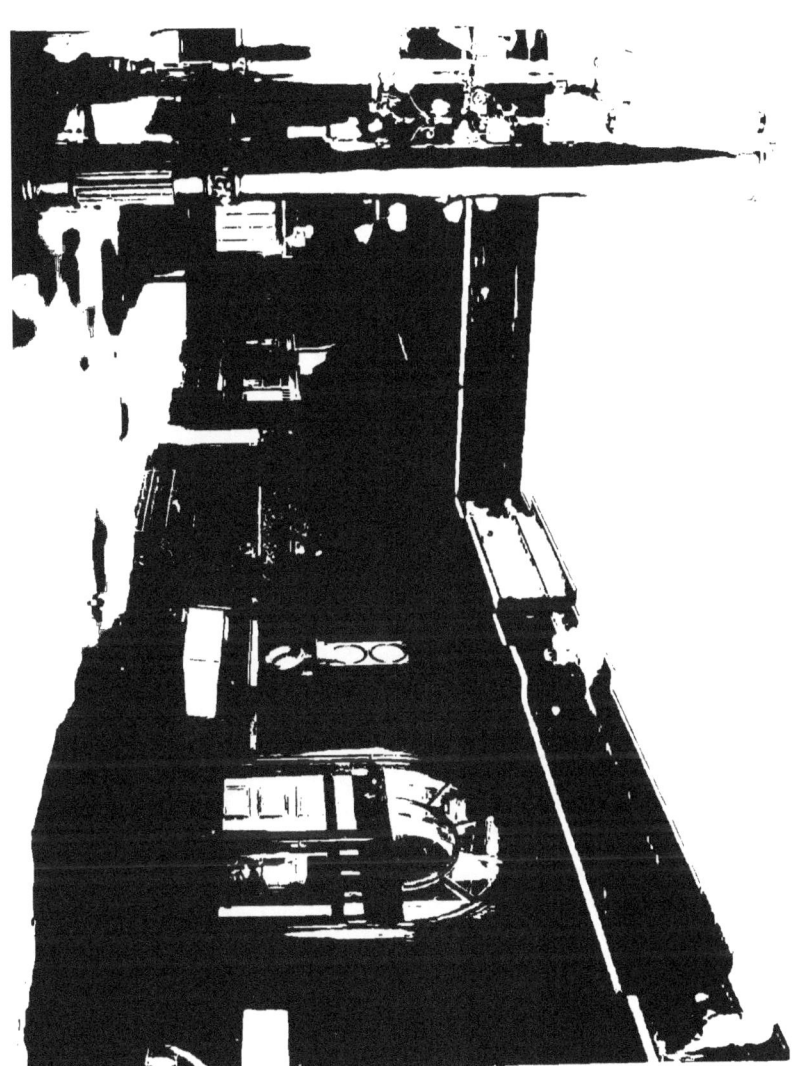

early as 1856 we begin to find complaint again in the annual reports of insufficient room for new books, and the talk of building reappears. The late George Palmer gave encouragement to the scheme that year by a munificent proposition. He offered to present to the Association a lot of land valued at $12,000, with $10,000 in money additional, provided that $90,000 more should be raised from other sources for an adequate building. The condition could not be fulfilled and the offered gift was lost. Next year the business world was strewn with the ruins of a financial earthquake. A little later came the political agitations which preceded the civil war, and then the war itself. There was little use in that period of talking or thinking about anything better for the library than the quarters which it had outgrown. Some growth went on, despite the tumult and despite the crowding. Just when the guns at Sumter were being trained to fire their war signal, on the evening of the 22d of March, 1861, the Association celebrated its quarter-centennial anniversary with stately ceremony and fine enthusiasm. The exercises, held in St. James Hall, were notably interesting. Mr. David Gray read a very noble poem, the strains of which are still lingering in the memory of those who heard it. Mr. Charles D. Norton delivered the historical address which has been quoted from above. Other addresses were made by Joseph Warren, then president of the Association, Hon. J. G. Masten, Hon. William Dorsheimer and Mr. Edward Stevens, with interludes of music, both vocal and instrumental.

These exercises were found so interesting and awakened so much life in the Association that something of like character was planned for the next annual meeting, held February 17, 1862. Again Mr. Gray contributed a memorable poem, while the late Judge Clinton delivered an admirable address, retrospective of events in the general history of the city.

Meantime, even amid the agitations of war, there occurred a revival of the dormant building project. It came to life in connection with the acceptance by the city of Buffalo of the bequest which founded the Grosvenor Library. Immediate efforts were set on foot to bring about a co-operative building undertaking looking to the permanent planting of the two libraries side by side. The original trustees of the Grosvenor Library, Messrs. O. H. Marshall, George R. Babcock, and J. G. Masten, were found to be favorable to the scheme. In the beginning it contemplated the acquisition, by gift from the city, of the old Mohawk street market-ground, (now the site of the Young Men's Christian Association building,) to be divided between the Young Men's Association and the Grosvenor Library, each to build upon its own part, but the contiguous buildings to be one in external unity. The undertaking looked hopeful for a time; then came various difficulties. Adjacent lots which were needed could not be reasonably bought, and some opposition to the Mohawk street location was found to exist. This was in 1862, when the war was at a gloomy crisis and national affairs were in a doubtful state. Yet, the executive committee of that year, with Gen. R. L. Howard at the head, were undaunted and persevering. They procured building subscriptions to an amount exceeding $10,000. They invited proposals for suitable building sites and reported nine offers, which were taken into consideration. One of these, which was for a lot of ground on Main street, above Huron, and opposite the North Church, gave so much satisfaction that the president, Gen. Howard, bought the property in his own name to secure it. The lot on the northerly side of Eagle street, fronting fifty-three feet on Main street and running to Washington street, was also proposed, Mr. S. V. R. Watson, who owned a half interest in the property, offering to make his interest a gift; but negotiations with owners of the adjacent ground to secure some necessary addition of space were not successful.

So the building project went over to the next year (1863), when Mr. S. V. R. Watson became president of the Association. Again there were many plans and many sites discussed, and several conferences were held by the building committee with the trustees of the Grosvenor Library and delegates from the Fine Arts Academy, the Historical Society, and the Society of Natural Sciences. The result was the provisional adoption of a 'plan contemplating the union of all the societies and the Grosvenor Library in the erection of a suitable building for their general accommodation, a specific part to be appropriated to each society, and the title of the premises to be vested in the Young Men's Association, except such part thereof as should be occupied by the Grosvenor Library.' But subsequently the Fine Arts Academy and Historical Society demanded modifications of the plan which the executive committee of the Y. M. A. 'deemed it would be unwise for this Association to adopt and it was thereafter abandoned.'

But, immediately on this, followed a movement which proved brilliantly successful, and which placed the library on sure ground for all time, as we may reasonably believe. President Watson opened negotiations with Messrs. Albert and George Brisbane for the purchase of the premises on Main, Eagle and Washington streets, known as the St. James Hotel and St. James Hall. Before the year closed, an agreement had been signed which secured three months' time for concluding the purchase of these premises at the price of $112,500. Within the stipulated three months, which expired March 26, 1864, a building fund amounting to $81,655 was raised by subscription among the members and friends of the Association, in sums which ranged from $5 to $3,000, and the purchase of the St. James Hotel and Hall property was duly consummated. A mortgage to the Erie County savings bank for $50,000 provided money for the completion of payments to the Messrs. Brisbane, and for the alterations required to be made in the premises. Possession of the hotel was secured September 1, and the necessary changes of interior construction were so speedily made that the library was formally installed in its new home on the 10th day of January, 1865. The occasion was distinguished by addresses from president Watson and from the late Oliver G. Steele, and by another poem from the pen of David Gray. It was the one, well remembered among Buffalonians, in which he paid his tender tribute to the brave McMahon, telling 'How the young Colonel died.'

In the reconstructed hotel building, the Association occupied the second floor with its library and reading-rooms, well accommodated. On the third, fourth and fifth floors suitable rooms were prepared for the Fine Arts Academy, the Historical Society and the Society of Natural Sciences, under an arrangement that was liberal in its terms. Soon afterwards the Grosvenor Library, then just beginning its collection of books, the Law Library, also in the infant stage, the Young Men's Christian Association, the Young Men's Catholic Association, the Erie County Medical Society and the Firemen's Benevolent Association were all given habitations in the hospitable building at moderate rates of rent. The Grosvenor Library was presently removed to other quarters, and several of the societies named were tenants for a few years only.

Four large stores on the ground floor of the building, and St. James

Hall at the rear, on Eagle and Washington streets, were leased on satisfactory terms, and brought in a handsome rental.

The Association was now very happy in its circumstances. Its library was well placed, with convenient arrangements and with space for a considerable growth. Its reading-rooms were commodious and pleasant. It had advanced in public favor and its membership increased. Its property, ably managed by three real-estate commissioners, yielded revenues which extinguished the mortgage debt upon it within thirteen years. At the same time the library enjoyed more liberal appropriations for books than had been possible before. Yet the accumulation of books was soon thought to be proceeding too slowly, and in 1869, under the presidency of Mr. Henry A. Richmond, a special fund for immediate purchases was provided by an issue of bonds. This gave to the library committees of the following two years nearly $19,000 for expenditure, and the total of books was raised from about 16,000 in 1870, to 25,000 in 1872, while a full and excellent catalogue was prepared and printed, supplying a want that had been urgent for many years.

The five years next following were not eventful in the life of the Association; but in 1877 an important amendment of its constitution was brought into effect. The object of the amendment was to cure the evil influence upon the library of an annual change in its administrative committees. Thereafter, the immediate supervision of the library was entrusted to three 'curators,' one elected each year, with two other members of the executive committee, appointed annually, forming a library committee; while the twelve directors in the executive committee were elected, four annually, for terms of three years each.

Soon afterwards, a change was made in the working organization of the library by creating the office of superintendent, Mr. J. N. Larned being appointed to the place and entering upon its duties in April, 1877. During that year and the following one, the library, which contained about 30,000 volumes at the beginning of the work, was reclassified and rearranged throughout on what is known as the 'movable system,' or 'system of relative location' for books, and a new card catalogue was made for the whole.

By the final extinction of the mortgage debt of the Association, at the beginning of 1878, a more continuous liberality of appropriations for the

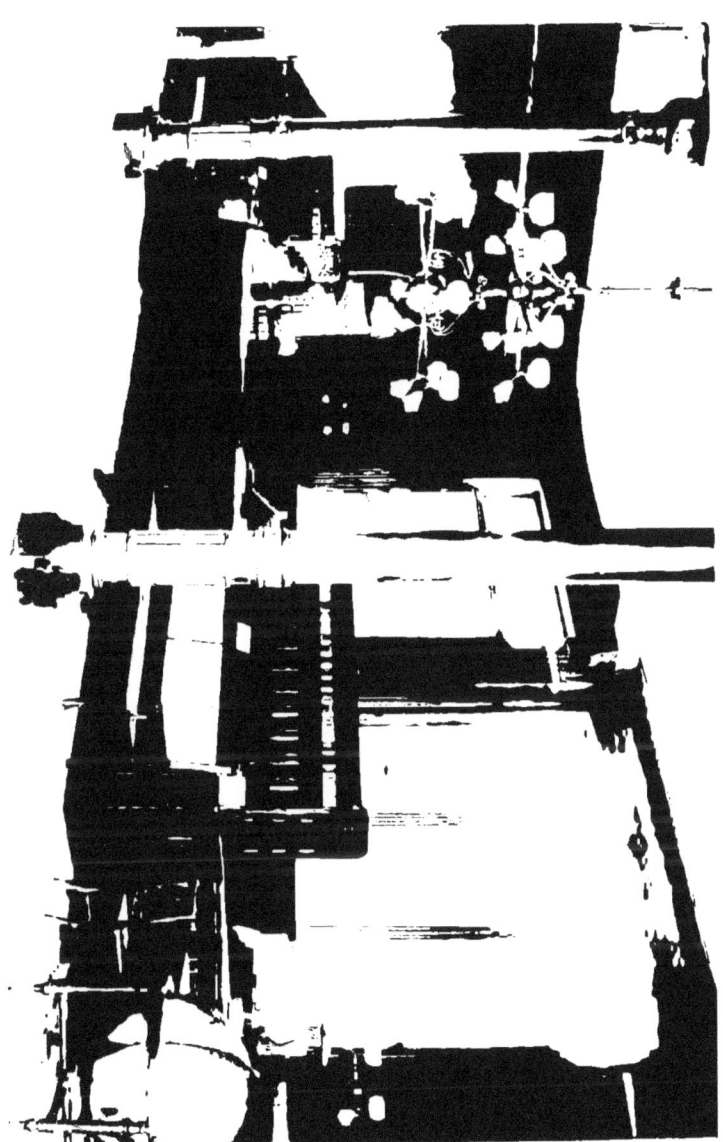

purchase of books was introduced from that date. Yet the total book expenditure of the succeeding ten years barely equalled that of the preceding decade, owing to the large extra fund that had been raised and applied in 1871 and 1872. In the ten years 1868-1877, 21,498 volumes of books were added to the library, and $37,200 expended. In the ten years 1878-1887, 29,224 volumes were added, and the expenditure was $37,139. This accelerated growth soon crowded the library shelves and forced extensions and changes of arrangement that were found every year more inconvenient and troublesome. At the same time, with the increasing value of the collection of books, an increasing desire was felt to see it more safely housed. Hence arose often recurring demands for the construction of a fire-proof library building. Attention had long been fixed upon the ground occupied by the old county buildings, vacated in 1876 (Washington, Broadway, Ellicott and Clinton streets), as offering the most desirable site, and several movements to secure the property were made, but with no result. In 1880 there was serious talk of purchasing the old Unitarian Church, at the corner of Franklin and Eagle streets, and converting it into a fire-proof structure for the library. Plans and estimates for the work were procured and considered, but the project did not meet with favor and was dropped. The suggested fire-proof reconstruction of the old church building was afterwards carried out by the Austin estate for business purposes.

In the autumn of 1882 a movement by various parties to bring about the sale of the county property mentioned above showed strong influence in the Board of Supervisors, and it appeared probable that the fine site in question would soon pass to private owners and be turned to some not very dignified commercial use. Hon. Sherman S. Rogers and Hon. James M. Smith, conversing on the subject one morning, resolved suddenly to rescue from that ignoble fate a piece of ground which seemed conspicuously designed for a worthy public edifice. They found seven other gentlemen to join them in forming a syndicate composed as follows: Sherman S. Rogers, James M. Smith, Sherman S. Jewett, Francis H. Root, Charles Berrick, O. P. Ramsdell, Dexter P. Rumsey, Pascal P. Pratt, Geo. Howard. These gentlemen, without delay, submitted proposals to the Board of Supervisors for the purchase of the ground in question, under agreement to transfer the same at any time within twelve months to any one or more of several societies and institutions named, which might determine to buy and build upon the site. Their proposal was accepted and the conveyance of the property was duly made to them.

The public spirit of the city was now challenged to make use of the opportunity thus secured. It was felt that the stipulated year must not be suffered to pass without determining an undertaking in some mode to cover the site worthily, and to gather there, if possible, under one stately roof, the representative institutions of art, science, and literature. The Young Men's Association was looked to for leadership in the enterprise. At the next election of the Association, in February, 1883, Mr. Edward B. Smith was chosen president, distinctly with a view to enlisting his known energy and resoluteness. Under Mr. Smith's command the campaign was soon opened. The trustees of the Grosvenor Library and the citizen's committee, or syndicate, which held the old court-house property, joined the officers of the Association in sending out to prominent citizens an invitation phrased as follows:

> A meeting of gentlemen will be held at 8 o'clock on Wednesday evening, April 18th, at the residence of Mr. Sherman S. Jewett, for the purpose of consultation respecting plans for the improvement of the old court-house lands, with a view to establishing the important art, literary, and scientific institutions of the city in a suitable edifice upon that most central and commanding site.
>
> We are permitted by Mr. Jewett to invite to this conference a few of the prominent citizens most likely to feel interest in the matter, and such invitation is respectfully extended to you. It is hoped you will not fail to be present.

The meeting was largely attended and gave a powerful impetus to the undertaking by its encouraging spirit. Mr. Smith submitted a plan of proceeding, which contemplated the co-operation of the Grosvenor Library with the Young Men's Association in the erection of a building, or of two buildings which might be substantially one in design, to accommodate not only themselves, but likewise the Fine Arts Academy, the Historical Society and the Society of Natural Sciences; the Young Men's Association to raise for the purpose about $175,000, by bonds and otherwise, the Grosvenor Library to expend its accumulated building fund of $65,000, and $100,000 or $125,000 additional to be procured by private subscriptions from the friends of the

enterprise. The plan was generally approved by the meeting, and resolutions were adopted which recommended the Association to enter upon the proposed undertaking with vigor, and at once. After the adjournment a subscription book was opened and headed with the signatures of Sherman S. Jewett and Sherman S. Rogers, with $5,000 attached to each.

From this auspicious beginning the subscription was pushed actively, but did not advance with the rapidity that might have been expected. The 1st of December found some $30,000 still wanting to make up the $100,000 which the terms of the subscription required to be raised before the end of that month. The prospect was discouraging, and not many men would have confronted it with the determination shown by president Smith. He had no thought of relinquishing the undertaking. Having apparently exhausted the subscriptions in large sums, or nearly so, he turned to the whole membership of the Association, and to the public at large, with a strong appeal for contributions of any and every amount within the means of the contributor. The response to this appeal was surprising. A single week changed the whole aspect of affairs. For sums ranging all the way from $1.00 to $500, subscriptions in amazing numbers were poured in, and the total footing reached and passed $100,000 some days before the close of the month. The final result was a building-fund subscription which aggregated about $117,000, nearly all of which proved eventually to be good.

The undertaking was now assured, and attention was promptly turned to the procuring of satisfactory designs and plans for the nascent edifice. The superintendent of the library was deputed to visit several eastern cities, to confer with leading architects and to study the construction and arrangements of the best library buildings. By the concurrent action of the executive committee and the board of real estate, a building committee of five was appointed, to which large powers were delegated, for the supervision and direction of the contemplated work. The committee was constituted as follows: Edward B. Smith, chairman, Jewett M. Richmond, John G. Milburn, George B. Hayes, J. N. Larned.

The first proceeding of the building committee was to open conferences and correspondence with the trustees of the Grosvenor Library and with the managing boards of the Fine Arts Academy, the Society of Natural Sciences, and the Historical Society. It was soon found that the trustees of the Grosvenor Library entertained views respecting the division of cost and of accommodations between the two libraries, and consequent plans of building, which differed so radically from the views held on the side of the Association that no possible reconciliation of them could be hoped for. All attempts, therefore, to arrange a co-operative enterprise were abandoned, and the Association addressed itself independently to the work. Little difficulty was found in arriving at an understanding with the three other societies expecting to be tenants of the building when completed. It was agreed with the Fine Arts Academy that rooms and sky-lighted galleries to cover not less than a certain designated area on the second floor should be provided 'for its uncontrolled use, during whatever period it may choose to occupy the same as an art-gallery, free of any rent-charge, but subject only to the conditions that it shall maintain the said portion of the building in proper repair and that it shall pay its proportion of the cost of warming the building.' With the Historical Society and the Society of Natural Sciences the agreement was for a tenancy on similar terms, but limited to twenty-five years in duration, after which time, or earlier if the premises in question should be vacated, 'the Association may reclaim the same.' Rooms for the Historical Society were to be not less than 4,500 square feet in area, on the third floor, and those for the Society of Natural Sciences in the basement, 10,000 square feet in area at the least.

Meantime — and long previously, in fact — careful studies were being made to determine the form of building and the arrangement of floor plans that would seem to satisfy the wants of the library and the demands of the associated group of institutions in the most perfect way. The peculiar trapezoidal lot of ground to be built upon offered difficulties and advantages, in equal measure, perhaps, and made the problem interesting. As the fruit of these studies, a set of floor-plan sketches was prepared, by way of suggestion to the architects who might undertake to submit designs for the building. (See opposite page.)

The architects of the city were all invited to offer competitive designs, and the same invitation was extended to thirteen architects in other cities. The middle of April had been reached before these invitations were sent out. To each architect invited there was sent a copy of the suggested floor plans mentioned above, together with a printed circular which described,

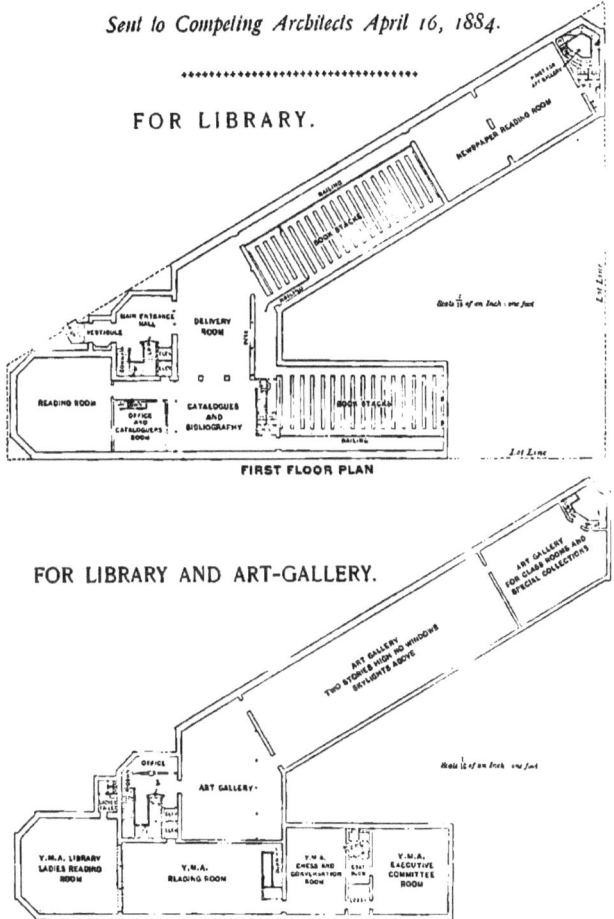

in full detail, all the wants to be satisfied and all the conditions to be met in the construction and arrangements of the building. 'The accompanying sketches,' it was said, 'are only intended to indicate in a more graphic way than can be done by any description the main features of arrangement that we seek to obtain in the proposed building. They are offered merely as the result of studies made by those who are best acquainted with the problems involved, but who are anxious that the invention of architects shall be exercised upon the same problems without trammel or bias from these suggestions.'

With reference to the important matter of the storage arrangement of books in the library, the specifications of the circular were precise. It called for 'a book-room, or rooms, capable of containing 200,000 to 250,000 volumes. In estimating capacity of book-rooms the calculation is to be 10 volumes to the running foot of shelf measure. Cases or stacks for books to be framed of iron, 18 inches through, and placed not less than 2 feet 8 inches apart. Unless there are objections found,' said the circular, 'which we do not now foresee, our preference is for a modified form of the book-stack system, as adopted in the library of Harvard University; so modified, that is, that the stacks shall not be raised above two stages or tiers of 7 feet each in height, and that there shall be, say, 7 clear feet of air space between the top of the stack and the ceiling of the room, thus permitting a third stage to be added in the future if desired. . . . The shelves to be in equal sections of three feet length. The arrangement for light to be carefully considered with reference to the long and narrow spaces into which it must penetrate.'

The limit of time named for receiving designs was July 1st. At the appointed date eleven architects were found to have submitted designs to the committee, but anonymously, as was prescribed. The eleven competitors, subsequently identified, were: H. H. Richardson, Brookline, Mass.; Van Brunt & Howe, Boston; C. L. W. Eidlitz, New-York; W. H. Wilcox, St. Paul, Minn.; William Watson, Montreal; Warner & Brockett, Rochester, N. Y.; C. K. Porter, Buffalo; Beebe and Freeman, Buffalo; August Esenwein and F. W. Humble, Buffalo; C. R. Percival, Buffalo; H. Macdiarmid, Buffalo.

After careful and long consideration, the building committee, on the 11th of July, adopted as its choice, with unanimity, the design submitted by

Mr. C. L. W. Eidlitz of New-York. At the same time, the second premium that had been offered was awarded to Mr. Richardson, and the third to Mr. Wilcox. The action of the committee was confirmed by the executive committee of the association, and it was unquestionably approved by the general public verdict.

Arrangements were now promptly concluded with Mr. Eidlitz for the preparation of working plans and specifications, and early in October a contract for the excavation and foundation work of the building was let. Ground was broken on the morning of the 8th of October, in the presence of a few ladies and gentlemen who had warning of the event, and who took the place of the laborers for a time in handling plough and shovel. The first wagon was loaded by these volunteers and the first spadeful of earth thrown into it by Mrs. S. V. R. Watson.

In January, 1885, the contracts for the principal work were let. At this time the building-plans contemplated a strictly fire-proof construction for only the Broadway wing of the building, in which the book-room of the library and the picture-gallery of the Fine Arts Academy were to be placed. No more than that could be done within the limit of $225,000 that had been fixed for the cost of construction. But further consideration led to a revision of these plans, and it was determined that the whole structure should be made fire-proof. Supplementary contracts were accordingly made, under which work began in April.

Mr. Smith had been re-elected president in February, 1884, but declined a third election the following year, pleading the pressure of his private business affairs upon his attention and time. He accepted, however, a seat in the board of real estate. His natural successor in the presidency was Mr. Jewett M. Richmond, who had been one of the building committee and prominently active in the whole movement. Mr. Richmond was re-elected in 1886 and again in 1887, and surrendered his services very largely to the undertaking, giving close personal attention to it throughout.

The vacancy in the building committee caused by the retirement of Mr. Smith (Mr. Richmond then becoming chairman of the committee) was filled by the appointment of Mr. Henry C. French. In the following year, 1886, Mr. French and Mr. Geo. B. Hayes were withdrawn from the building committee by the expiration of their terms in the executive committee, and were succeeded by Messrs. Howard H. Baker and Robert R. Hefford.

As the building progressed and contracts were let, the work in its various parts, from beginning to completion, was executed and directed as follows:

Architect, ... CYRUS L. W. EIDLITZ.
Architect's superintendent, ... AUG. ESENWEIN.

CONTRACTORS.

Excavation and foundations,	J. BEIER & SON.
Mason work (superstructure),	CHAS. BERRICK.
Stone work (superstructure),	W. COLLINGWOOD.
Iron work,	H. C. HARROWER.
Terra cotta,	BOSTON TERRA COTTA CO.
Carpenter work,	JACOB REIMANN.
Painting and finishing,	D. F. RUST.
Roofing,	G. H. PETERS & SON.
Steam heating and plumbing,	IRLBACKER & DAVIS.
Steam boiler house,	CHAS. BERRICK.
Book stacks,	H. C. HARROWER.
Sandstone sidewalks,	BRADY & MALTBY.
Oak wainscoting, cases, tables, etc.,	METZ, BARK & MEYER.
Chairs,	HERSEE & CO.
Frescoing,	C. F. CHRETIEN & BROS.
Light fixtures (gas and electric combination),	IRLBACKER & DAVIS.
Tiling,	L. SCHWARTZ & CO.
Floor covering ("noiseless corticine"),	D. MORGAN & SON.
Speaking tubes and electric bells,	CHAS. PLUMB.
Electric lighting,	U. S. ELECTRIC LIGHT CO.

Work was pressed vigorously by most of the contractors, but lasted through 1885, 1886, and until March, 1887, before the last details were finished.

In May, 1886, by an act of the Legislature of New-York, the 'Young Men's Association of Buffalo' became, by change of name, 'The Buffalo Library,' and its 'executive committee' was changed in title to a 'board of managers.'

On Monday, the 13th of September, 1886, the removal of the library to its new home was begun. The new building was not yet in readiness for it, but the old building was no longer hospitable. The latter had been

leased to Messrs. Stafford & Co. for reversion to its original uses as a hotel. Extensive changes of interior construction required to be made, and the commencement of work upon these necessarily hastened the departure of the library. As an unfortunate consequence, its books were put out of use for nearly four months. It was not until the third day of January, 1887, that the stately portals on Broadway could be opened to readers.

Even then the opening was informal and incomplete. The ceremonious and official introduction of the public to the new building was postponed until the evening of Monday, February 7th, when the Library united with the Fine Arts Academy, the Historical Society and the Society of Natural Sciences, in a general reception of their members and friends. A prayer by Bishop Coxe, brief addresses by president Richmond of the Library, vice-president Sherman S. Rogers of the Fine Arts Academy, president D. S. Kellicott of the Society of Natural Sciences, and ex-president James Sheldon of the Historical Society, with a short reminiscent sketch by Mr. John R. Lee, the first treasurer of the Young Men's Association, and the only survivor of its first board of officers, were the simple dedicatory exercises that had been prepared. Notwithstanding unfavorable weather, the guests of the evening numbered many thousands, and the splendid building, thronged in every part, presented a memorable scene. A programme of music, performed by the Philharmonic Orchestra, gave appropriate entertainment to the visitors.

The library at this time was fully settled and arranged; the other institutions were not. The Fine Arts Academy gave its opening exhibition a few weeks later; but it was not until June that the exhibition rooms of the Society of Natural Sciences were in order.

So far as the chronicle of the Buffalo Library can now be written it closes with a terrible incident. In the early morning of the 18th day of March, 1887, the building which it had vacated the preceding September, and which (still owned by the library) had become "The Richmond" hotel, was consumed by fire and fifteen persons perished in the flames or died from injuries received in escaping. The horrible calamity has cast a great shadow upon what had seemed to be the happy fortunes of the institution, and in this writing of its history we are compelled to leave it with that shadow still dark. It has been determined already, however, that a new hotel building, of strictly fire-proof construction, shall be erected without delay upon the site of the one destroyed, and that the Library will own it.

THE BUILDING.

The accompanying plans show the form of the building and the arrangement and allotment of its several floors, as constructed. The plans, it will be seen, are drawn nearly on the lines suggested at the beginning by the studies of the building committee. In a communication which accompanied his drawings when first submitted, Mr. Eidlitz wrote:

> The plans prepared by you for the use of competitors and the printed programme of requirements have been made the basis of this design. They have not, however, been adopted without careful scrutiny and the undertaking of many independent studies. These studies have had the result of confirming the impression that no disposition essentially different from that arrived at by you could, under the conditions of the site and the limit of cost, be made to meet so well the varied requirements of your enterprise.

Mr. Eidlitz, however, introduced a change of great importance in the plans. By widening the Broadway wing of the building he made room there for the entire book-storage required, and then secured the necessary increase of light demanded for the widened book-room by narrowing a part of the art-gallery above, which permitted skylights to be placed on each side of it. This construction not only improved the arrangement for book-storage but formed a striking and pleasing feature in the architecture of the building.

THE BOOK ROOMS.

The wing in question, on the library floor, is divided by heavy walls with large open arches into what may be called three rooms, or three sections of one room. It is 47 feet wide and 132 feet long, about one fourth of the total length being in each of the end sections, and one half

BUFFALO LIBRARY AND ART BUILDING.

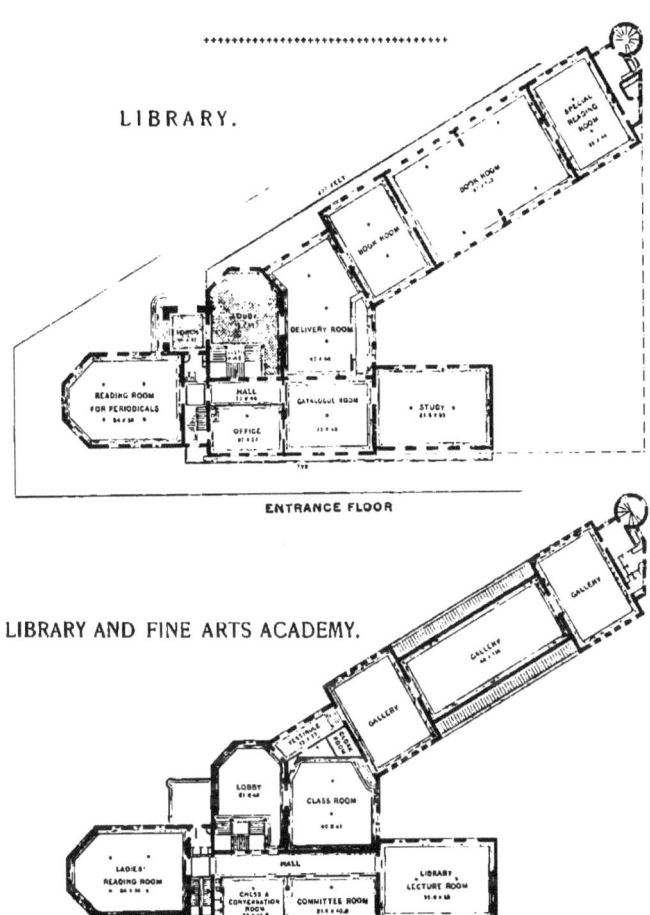

BUFFALO LIBRARY AND ART BUILDING.

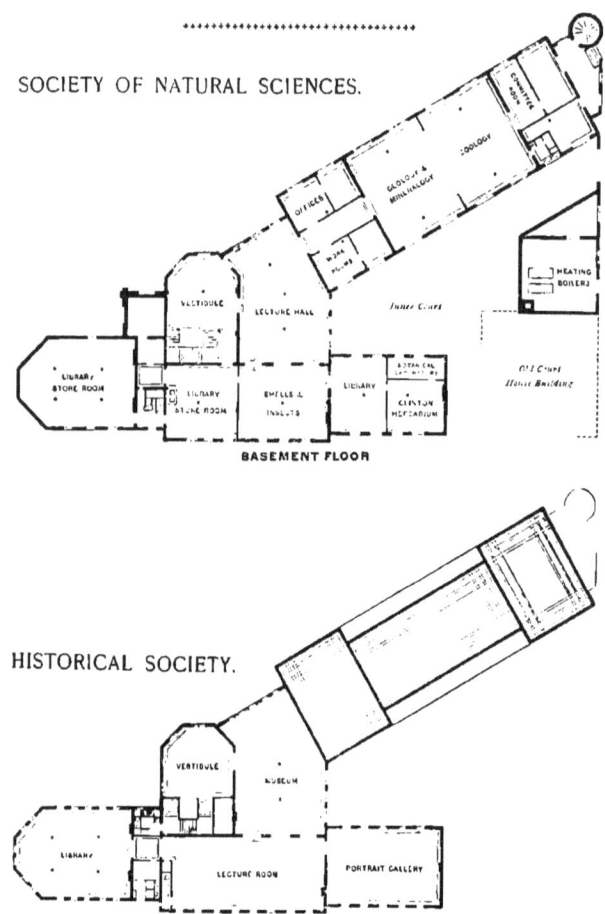

of it in the middle section. All these sections may be filled with bookstacks when needed. At present there are book-stacks erected in the middle and westerly sections only. The book-stacks are but two stages of seven feet each in height. The room having a height of 22 feet, from floor to ceiling, it is possible, at any time, to add a third tier to the stacks. As now constructed their capacity is for holding something more than 150,000 volumes. If extended into the easterly section of the room and carried up to a third stage throughout, that capacity will be very nearly doubled. In his recent annual report the superintendent of the library, speaking of the provision for future accumulations of books, stated the facts as follows: 'We can double their present number and then double it again without filling, by 50,000 books, the space, even now appropriated to them. When that is done there will still remain the great halls which the Art Gallery, the Society of Natural Sciences and the Historical Society will some day vacate, and which are ample for the storing of full twice as many more, with reading-rooms proportionately supplied. In a word, the Buffalo Library may grow, in some far future time, to the imperial magnitude of a million books without going outside of its present walls.'

Supporting nothing but their own weight, with that of the books which they carry, the stacks are of a simple and light construction. Thin cast-iron cross-pieces, or bearings, slide upon standards of one-inch gas pipe, being adjustably fixed in place by steel set-screws, and these are flanged for holding the shelves. The platform which constitutes the floor to the second stage is of light iron gratings and rough glass in about equal proportions. The stacks are 15 feet long, each divided into five shelf-sections of three feet each. They are 18 inches in depth, from face to face, thus giving a shelf nine inches wide on each face, and there is no partition between these two opposed shelves. The passage between the stacks is 32 inches wide, and this is found to be quite sufficient.

There are two rows of these stacks, with a broad passage enclosed within iron railings carried down through the middle of the room between them. The passage is bridged to establish easy communication from one row of book-stacks to the other. The purpose of this passage-way is to give public entrance to the large room at the easterly end of the book-stacks, which will not be needed for book storage until many years hence, and which is important for other uses in the meantime. It has been proposed that this commodious and very light reading-room, together with the book-stacks on the northerly side of the contiguous book-room, be occupied by the Grosvenor Library until such time as that institution is prepared to erect a building of its own. But nothing to the purpose has been arranged. At present the room is for teachers who bring classes to the library, for students who wish to consult a great number of books, and for other special uses of that character.

THE DELIVERY ROOM.

The delivery room, which is the *foyer* of the library, where everything centers, and from which everything radiates, is an apartment of fine proportions, with irregular form, and produces a striking effect upon the visitor when he enters. Being really continuous with the adjoining catalogue-room, from which it is separated only by the piers of three wide, round arches, the appearance is of an extended hall crossing the building from street to street, 104 feet long and 40 feet wide. The walls are frescoed in plain designs, but in rich, dark colors, Venetian red predominant, and this harmonizes finely with the antique, quartered oak wood-work and furniture. The abundance of light in the rooms, from two wide streets and from the large court behind, supports and enriches these dark colors, which would not be admissible without it.

The delivery-desk faces the entrance to the room — which is the one public entrance to the library — and behind it are wide, high windows opening into the court. At the left of the entrance, going in, are the cases containing the remarkable collection of autograph manuscripts and letters presented to the library by Mr. James Frazer Gluck, with some others from other donors. To the right is the catalogue room, through which one passes to reach the general reading rooms and the office.

THE CATALOGUE ROOM.

This room contains the card catalogue of the library, in drawers which are at one level, and which are covered with hinged lids, so that the use

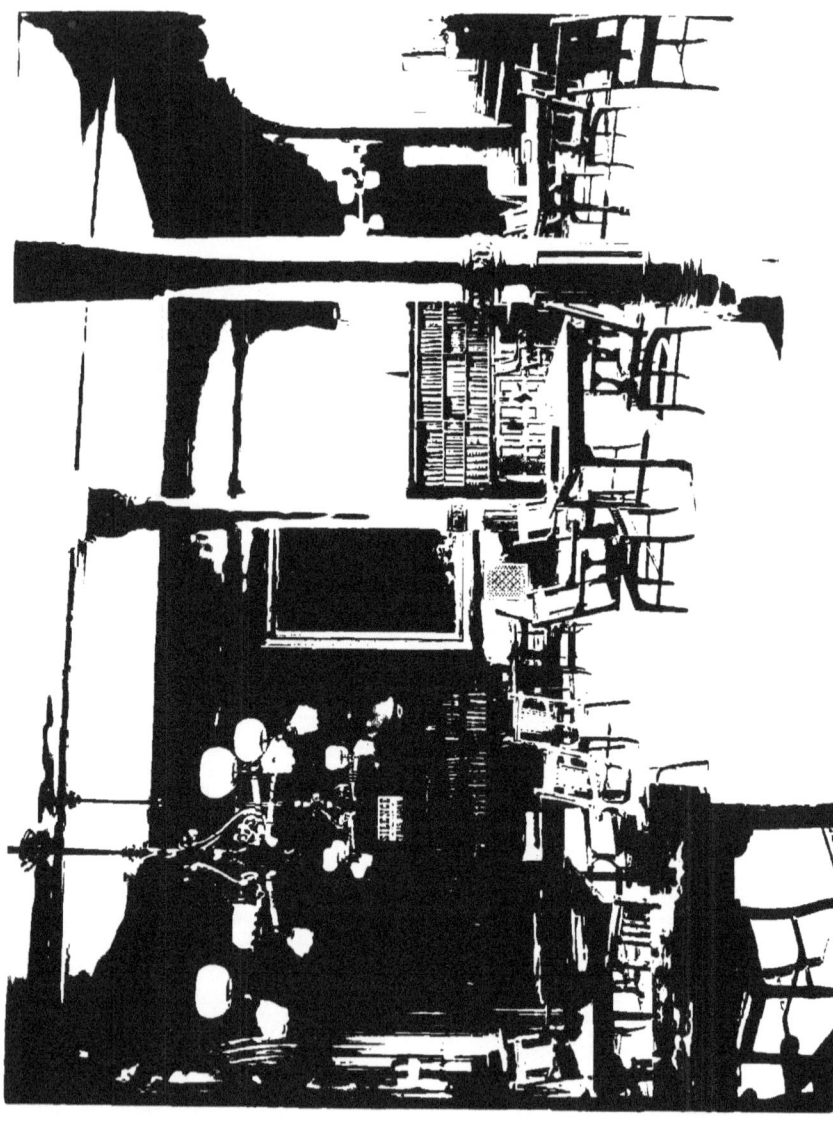

of one interferes with no other. All bibliographical books, and such few rare and curious books as the library now possesses, with its collection of texts and versions of the Bible (just fairly begun) are also here, in fine oak cases, behind glass. For the present, the collections of the library in local history and literature are likewise placed in this room.

THE STUDY.

At the rear of the catalogue room is 'The Study,' or reference reading-room, which we pass into through silent swinging doors, half crystal with plate glass in beveled squares. It is full of light from windows on its two longest sides, opening to the street on one hand, and to the large inner court on the other. The room is 52 feet long by 33½ feet wide. Its colors are soft and warm. It is well filled but not crowded with tables and chairs. At each end of it are open cases in which a thousand volumes or more of the commoner books of reference — encyclopædias, dictionaries, gazetteers, statistical annuals, and the like — are placed for free use. Other reference books are with the general library in the book-room, and subject to call.

READING-ROOM FOR PERIODICALS.

Passing in the opposite direction from the catalogue-room, through a broad hall, the reading-room for newspapers and magazines is reached. It occupies entirely the large bay in the front of the building, 54 feet by 38 feet in size, and has windows on three sides of it, looking out on wide, open spaces of ground. In the fourth wall, at either hand on entering, are two great fire-places and chimney pieces of terra cotta, which help much to give a pleasant aspect to the place. In the middle of the room is a case of peculiar design, having drawers below and open compartments above, on each of its long sides. The compartments are of different sizes for periodicals of every description, daily newspapers included, each one lettered for its own. Few files are used, but every newspaper is stitched at the back by a sewing machine and laid flatly, or with a single fold, in its place. When necessary the paper is stitched upon a strip of tape to strengthen it. Only a few of the latest numbers are left out in the open case, the older numbers being filed away daily in the drawers below for reference. A lady attendant has charge of the room and re-arranges the periodicals as often as they are displaced. The reading-room is frequented by both ladies and gentlemen, and, though it is entirely free and almost constantly filled, perfect order and perfect quiet are preserved in it.

THE LADIES' ROOM.

Although every other reading-room is open to ladies as well as to gentlemen, the former are additionally provided with a reading-room of more privacy for their exclusive use. As it naturally should be, the ladies' room is the most beautiful in the building and the most choicely situated. It is on the second floor, in the front, immediately above the reading-room for periodicals just described. It has the same dimensions as that and is correspondingly open to light and air, the prospect from several of its windows being singularly fine. Its floor is made soft with rugs, and it is furnished with the most comfortable of chairs. A lady attendant is always present in the room.

AUTOGRAPH MANUSCRIPT COLLECTION.

The cases shown in one of the views of the 'delivery-room,' standing at the northerly end of the apartment, contain a collection of autograph manuscripts and letters which is probably unequalled in America. Excepting a few contributions from other sources, the collection was made for the library by one of its present curators, Mr. James Frazer Gluck. Many of the manuscripts were purchased by Mr. Gluck and many were given for the collection, by authors and publishers, at his request. The total number is between three hundred and four hundred, of which more than half are singly bound in sumptuous volumes. Some are collectively bound, and others, among the shorter manuscripts and letters, are framed in oak.

The autographs in the collection which receive the most attention, perhaps, and are most interesting to the majority of people, are the following: The entire original manuscripts of Emerson's 'Representative Men'; of Parkman's 'Count Frontenac and New France'; of William Cullen

Bryant's Introduction to the Odyssey; Gladstone's essay on 'England and Russia'; Lowell's essay on 'The Winthrop Papers'; Whittier's 'The King's Missive'; Dickens' 'Great International Walking Match'; Mark Twain's 'Huckleberry Finn'; one of Bret Harte's 'Condensed Novels' and 'Por el Rey'; Thoreau's essay on 'Mortal Glory'; Hazlitt's lecture on 'Dryden and Pope'; Walt Whitman's essay on 'Robert Burns'; Leigh Hunt's criticism of Carlyle's first lectures in London; Sir Thos. Overbury's 'Observations upon the Seventeen Provinces,' A. D. 1609; one of Charles Kingsley's lectures; one of Tom Moore's songs with the music; one of Chancellor Kent's Opinions; one of Helen Hunt's 'Bits of Travel'; parts of the autograph manuscripts of Sir Walter Scott's essay on 'Chivalry,' of Southey's 'The Doctor,' and of Cooper's 'The Headsman'; a volume of Watts' Hymns, in his handwriting; single autograph poems by Dryden, Dorset, Burns, Wordsworth, Keats, Coleridge, Hood; a volume of Tennyson's proof-sheets as he corrected them; a volume of De Quincey's proof-sheets and letters; a volume of Browning's and Mrs. Browning's letters; characteristic and important single letters by Washington, Jefferson, Franklin, Lincoln, Hawthorne, Poe, Voltaire, Rousseau, Jeremy Taylor, Dr. Johnson, Pope, Cowper, Macaulay, Ruskin, George Eliot, Charles Lamb, etc., etc.

MINOR DETAILS.

On the same floor with the ladies' reading-room are the board of managers' room, a small lecture-room, seating about 225 people, and a room assigned to chess playing.

The office, on the main floor, is conveniently arranged for the administrative work of the library. Below it, and connected by stairway and bookhoist, are well-lighted packing and storage-rooms in the basement.

The entire wood fittings and furniture of the library are of quartered oak, antique in finish, and highly polished. The cases, desks and tables were carefully planned, in dimensions, arrangement and place, by the superintendent of the library, and designed by the architect.

The library floors are generally covered with "noiseless corticine," a material which seems to be admirably adapted to library use. It preserves as much quiet in the rooms as carpeting would do, while it can be washed like a wood floor. Laid down in its natural brown color, with no pattern printed on the surface, it looks well, even after much wear.

The incandescent electric light and gas light, in combination fixtures, are introduced together throughout the library rooms. If one fails, the other is at hand; but the electric light is the one commonly in use.

Every room communicates with every other by speaking tubes and electric signals.

The warming of the building is by steam, from boilers placed in a house entirely detached, at the rear.

THE FINE ARTS ACADEMY.

The Fine Arts Academy.

N the second floor of the northerly or Broadway wing of the building, but extending up through two stories to the roof, are the galleries of the Fine Arts Academy. Those at each end are about 47 by 33 feet in dimensions, while the longer and narrower gallery between them is 68 feet long by 31½ feet wide. All are skylighted from the roof through ceilings of thick glass. At the time the view shown in this book was taken, the galleries were unfinished and slightly furnished.

Connected with the galleries is an art school-room 40 by 41 feet in size.

In his address at the opening of the building, February 7, 1887, Hon. Sherman S. Rogers gave the following brief historical sketch of the origin and growth of the Academy:

When the future historian, writing of our great civil war, and looking for truth more in the deeds of the time than in its talk, shall inquire as to the spirit and temper of the north in those days of defeat and humiliation, I think he may find one of some significance in this: that on the 8th day of November, 1862, a few of our leading citizens founded the Buffalo Fine Arts Academy.

I confess to a feeling of pride as I recall the fact that its first president was my own honored and beloved kinsman, Henry W. Rogers. Would you know the spirit with which the enterprise was started? Let me read to you from the address of Mr. Sellstedt, read at the annual opening ten years later. There was immediate need of money, and Messrs. Rogers and Hazard were appointed a committee to obtain it. 'They started on their mission,' says

Mr. Sellstedt, 'on the morning of the 11th of December and before 6 P. M. had twelve subscribers of $500. They afterwards obtained one more, making the whole amount $6,500.' Could we do much better to-day? 'Would you know,' Mr. Sellstedt continues, 'the names of the Guard of Honor? They are Henry W. Rogers, George S. Hazard, Sherman S. Jewett, David S. Bennett, Bronson C. Rumsey, Charles Ensign, Chandler J. Wells, John Allen, Jr., Lauren C. Woodruff, Pascal P. Pratt, Stephen V. R. Watson, Francis H. Root and James Brayley.'

The formal inauguration of the academy took place on the 23d of December of the same year. Mr. Rogers held his office for two years. Mr. George S. Hazard succeeded him. From 1869 to 1871 Mr. Rogers was again president, and the office has also been filled by Sherman S. Jewett, Eben. P. Dorr, C. F. S. Thomas, William P. Letchworth, Sherman S. Rogers, Laurentius G. Sellstedt, John Allen, Jr., Josiah Jewett and Dr. Thomas F. Rochester.

Josiah Humphrey, A. M. Farnham and L. G. Sellstedt have filled the office of corresponding secretary, and H. Ewers Talmadge and Albert T. Chester that of recording secretary. Dr. Chester's service extends from 1864 to the present time, and it may be safely said that with the exception of Mr. Sellstedt no member of the executive board has rendered so much or so valuable service.

At the first our art possessions were very cheerfully and pleasantly housed in the Arcade block, on the northeast corner of Main and Clinton streets; afterward in the room so kindly provided us by the Young Men's Association in the building they have just vacated, and still later in the Austin fire-proof building on Eagle and Franklin opposite the city hall. The academy had begun to think it could not afford to be burned out. And now, at last, we are moving 'Laramie Peaks' and 'the Bay of Capri' and the rest of our treasures, together with some fine old trumpery which we cannot yet spare, into this welcome, thrice welcome home of letters and science and art. Here we trust they may remain until the greater Buffalo which we see yonder in the first quarter of the twentieth century shall need our rooms for the overflowing library, and a secure home shall have been provided for them in a temple of art worthy of a great and generous city.

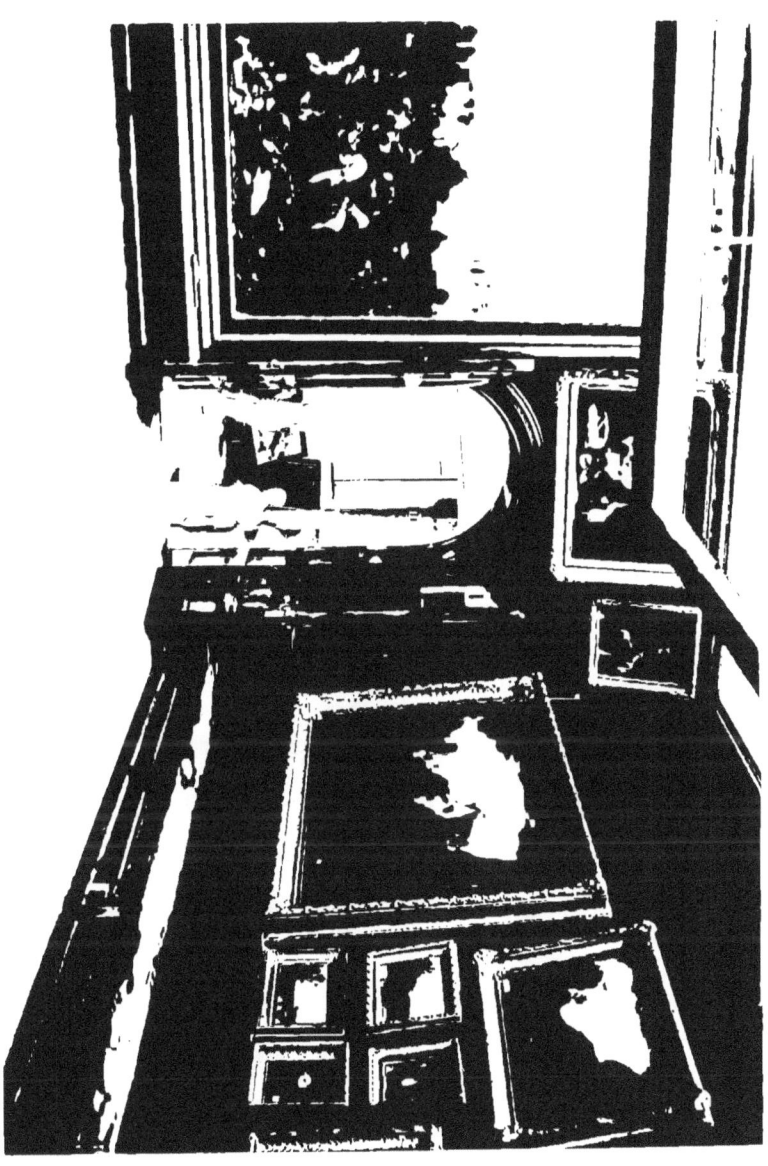

SOCIETY OF NATURAL SCIENCES.

THE SOCIETY OF NATURAL SCIENCES.

LTHOUGH the spacious rooms of the Society of Natural Sciences are in the basement of the building, they lie nearly at the ground level throughout most of their extent, owing to the slope on which the building stands. The light in them is perfect, and the museum, the laboratories, the library, and the offices of the Society are excellently accommodated.

The important incidents in the history of the society were briefly touched upon, and the chief treasures among its collections were pointed out, by the president, Prof. Kellicott, in his address at the opening of the building:

> It may be known to you, he said, that the society has just completed twenty-five years of existence, and it seems well that I should revert briefly to what it has accomplished during its first quarter of a century. I shall not weary you with an attempt at a history of its achievements; if this was the occasion, I am not the one properly to do it, for there are those with us who have known and aided it from the beginning; those whose names appear on the first page of its proceedings. It is for some one of these to write our history, not only from the records, but from experience and personal knowledge. The first page of the minutes contains the following: 'Buffalo, December 5, 1861; Tuesday evening. Pursuant to a call through the papers those interested in and connected with the formation of the society met in lower St. James Hall for the purpose of organization. Judge Clinton in the chair and T. Howland secretary. The meeting being called to order was addressed by Judge Clinton, and remarks were made by

Dr. Clarke, Havens and others.' After the reading and adoption of rules for government, officers were nominated and elected. This is the list:

OFFICERS.

President, HON. GEORGE W. CLINTON; *First Vice-President*, A. T. CHESTER, D. D.; *Second Vice-President*, CHARLES WINNE, M. D.; *Corresponding Secretary*, SAMUEL SLADE; *Recording Secretary*, THEODORE HOWLAND; *Treasurer*, LEON F. HARVEY, M. D.; *Librarian*, RICHARD K. NOYE.

CURATORS.

General Zoology, GEORGE E. HAYES, M. D.; *Ornithology*, Prof. WILLIAM S. VAN DUZEE; *Herpetology and Ichthyology*, HIRAM E. TALLMADGE; *Entomology*, CHARLES D. MARSHALL; *Conchology*, COLEMAN T. ROBINSON; *Botany*, C. C. F. GAY, M. D.; *Geology*, CHARLES S. FARNHAM; *Palæontology*, DAVID F. DAY.

Judge Clinton remained the president of the society until his removal to Albany in 1881. His virtues as a citizen, his devotion to the society and to the advancement of science, are too well known to need repetition here. It is conceded that the success of the society is largely due to his spirit and his labors. The record of his investigations on the flora of this vicinity must remain forever an honor to him, a benefit to all students of our plants and a heritage of the society. Our extensive collection of plants, now known as the Clinton Herbarium, is the result of years of untiring industry, and appropriately bears the name of its author. I may add that it is the only collection of plants within reach of the general student of botany in this city.

The first president was succeeded by Dr. George E. Hayes, himself one of the first curators and a constant supporter of the society while he lived; by his will he endowed it with a larger amount than was ever given by an individual to scientific associations in America. The bequest of Dr. Hayes renders it possible in the future for this society to take rank with those of Boston and Philadelphia. He has established a perpetual free school of science in Buffalo, to be administered by the society. Coleman T. Robinson and Charles F. Wadsworth, curators at the first organization, have both contributed large amounts to the society's possessions and largely to its standing. The latter left it the Wadsworth collection of minerals, which is indeed a treasure; first for its intrinsic value as a carefully selected collection; second, because it is within reach of our students and is the only one thus accessible. The former left us by will his library and the greater part of the present available invested funds. The valuable library thus begun has been increased by purchase and by exchange for the bulletin of the

society, until local students of science find here the means of investigation found nowhere else in western New-York. I will take the time to mention another matter which lends interest and value to this collection of books. I shall not be disputed, I think, in the assertion that more original descriptions of insects have been founded upon and referred to the identical books of this library than to any other collection in America. I refer to the descriptions by C. T. Robinson, A. R. Grote, L. F. Harvey and others.

There are other valuable collections which can scarcely be more than mentioned. For example, that of local birds; by it our students may identify almost every species taken here; the beautiful collection of European birds purchased, I am told, by subscription of the board of managers at a regular meeting; then the waterlime fossils, the finest in any collection; the collection of shells and others deserve mention but must be omitted. Their money value I dare not attempt to express. Now that they are stored in a fireproof building there is relief from anxiety.

THE BUFFALO HISTORICAL SOCIETY.

THE BUFFALO HISTORICAL SOCIETY.

 A MEETING of fourteen gentlemen, held in the law office of the late O. H. Marshall, on the evening of the 25th of March, 1862, was the beginning of the Buffalo Historical Society. They were Orsamus H. Marshall, George W. Clinton, Henry W. Rogers, George R. Babcock, Oliver G. Steele, James P. White, Walter Clarke, Henry Lovejoy, William Dorsheimer, Albert L. Baker, Joseph Warren, David F. Day, Edward S. Rich and John Howcutt. They appointed a committee of seven to report a plan of organization, and the report was made to a larger and more public meeting, held April 15th, at the rooms of the Medical Association. At that meeting, and at a subsequent election, on the first Tuesday in May, the organization of the society was perfected and its officers chosen, with the Hon. Millard Fillmore, ex-President of the United States, in the presiding seat.

The first librarian and corresponding secretary was genial and gentle Guy H. Salisbury—the Charles Lamb of early Buffalo—who gave most of his time for a considerable period to the gathering and arranging of the society's primary collections. He was succeeded by Dr. William K. Scott, who held the post until 1867, when Dr. George S. Armstrong was called to fill it. Dr. Armstrong was librarian and secretary for more than twelve years, and resigned in 1879. His successors have been Rev. Albert Bigelow, 1879-1881, Elias O. Salisbury, 1881-1883, and George G. Barnum since the latter date.

The collections of the society were deposited for some time in the office of Hon. William Dorsheimer, where its meetings were also held. From 1865 to 1873 it had rooms in the building of the Young Men's Association. In January of the latter year it removed to the Western Savings Bank building, of which it occupied the entire third floor until January, 1887, when it took possession of the fine rooms provided for it in the new building of the Buffalo Library.

As shown by the latest report of the librarian, Mr. Barnum, the library of the society now contains 9,360 volumes of books; 769 volumes of newspapers; 7,570 pamphlets; 689 maps, charts and volumes of maps; 118 manuscripts and 23 manuscript vols.; 291 framed portraits, including 64 in oil; 805 portrait photographs, in albums; 334 views, etc., framed and in portfolios; 4 vols. of autograph letters, etc. The collections of the society in historical relics and mementoes are extensive and valuable. Battle-flags and trophies of the Revolution, the War of 1812, the Mexican War, the Canadian Patriot War, and the Rebellion; remains of the mound-builders and the Indians; relics of the pioneers of Western New-York and of the early navigators of the lakes; coins, medals and curios from many countries and times, form a museum of the most interesting character. The "Francis Memorials" of the Rebellion, collected by the late Julius Francis at a cost, it is said, of $20,000, are a rare feature of the collections. The library of the late John C. Lord, D. D., is soon to be placed in the keeping of the society by the city, to which it was willed.

APPENDIX.

OFFICIAL REGISTER

OF THE YOUNG MEN'S ASSOCIATION, NOW THE BUFFALO LIBRARY, 1836-1887.

++++++++++++++++++++++++++++++++++++

ABBREVIATIONS.—*C.*, Curator of the Library; *C. S.*, Corresponding Secretary; *D.*, Director, or Manager; *P.*, President; *R. E. C.*, Real Estate Commissioner; *R. S.*, Recording Secretary; *T.*, Treasurer; *V. P.*, Vice-President.

ADAMS, J. C., *D.* 1887.
ALBERGER, F. A., *D.* 1846.
ALBERGER, W. C., *D.* 1860.
ALLEN, G. W., *D.* 1836.
ALLEN, J. JR., *D.* 1863, 1864, 1865.—*V. P.* 1866.
ALLEN, W. K., *T.* 1867, 1868, 1873, 1874, 1875, 1877.—*D.* 1879, 1880.—*V. P.* 1881.
ATWATER, S. T., *D.* 1839.—*V. P.* 1845.—*P.* 1846.
AUSTIN, B. H., *D.* 1857, 1860, 1861, 1869, 1871.

BACON, E. R., *D.* 1871.—*C. S.* 1872.
BAKER, A. L., *D.* 1851.
BAKER, CLIFFORD A., *D.* 1859.
BAKER, H. H., *D.* 1867, 1871, 1884.—*P.* 1874.—*V. P.* 1885, 1886.—*R. E. C.* 1875, 1876, 1877.
BARCLAY, W. H., *D.* 1870.
BARKER, GEO. P., *D.* 1866.
BARNARD, A. J., *D.* 1868.
BARNARD, ALBERT, *D.* 1848, 1849.
BASS, L. K., *C. S.* 1862.—*R. S.* 1863, 1864.—*D.* 1868.—*V. P.* 1870.
BEALS, P. P., *D.* 1880, 1881, 1882.
BELL, DAVID, *D.* 1867, 1869.—*P.* 1873.
BENNETT, NATHANIEL, *D.* 1840.
BENNETT, THOS., *D.* 1843.
BENTLEY, G. T., *R. S.* 1861.—*D.* 1862, 1866.
BEYER, WM. H., *D.* 1870.
BISHOP, A. W., *D.* 1859, 1860.

BISSELL, HERBERT P., *C.* 1887.
BISSELL, W. S., *D.* 1874, 1877, 1878, 1879.—*P.* 1880.—*R. E. C.* 1883, 1884, 1885.
BLISS, J. H., *D.* 1851, 1853.—*R. S.* 1852.—*V. P.* 1854.
BOARDMAN, JNO., *D.* 1856.—*C. S.* 1857.
BOWEN, D. A., *D.* 1851.
BOWEN, DENNIS, *V. P.* 1847.
BRAYLEY, JAS., *D.* 1863, 1864.
BRISTOL, C. C., *V. P.* 1838.—*D.* 1840, 1849.
BROWN, GEO., *V. P.* 1836.
BROWN, GEO. P., *D.* 1848.
BROWN, JNO. S., *C. S.* 1841.
BROWN, MATTHEW, JR., *D.* 1841.
BRYANT, I. F., *D.* 1848, 1849.—*C. S.* 1850, 1851.
BRYANT, WARREN, *D.* 1839.—*V. P.* 1840.—*P.* 1841.
BRYANT, WM. C., *D.* 1867.
BULL, HENRY, *C. S.* 1867, 1868.—*R. S.* 1870.—*D.* 1875.—*V. P.* 1877.—*P.* 1882.
BULL, J. B., *T.* 1840, 1841.—*V. P.* 1843.—*P.* 1844.
BURCH, J. H., *T.* 1836.
BURCHARD, E., *D.* 1841.
BURROWS, R. L., *R. S.* 1851.—*C. S.* 1853.—*D.* 1855.—*V. P.* 1857.
BURT, H. W., *T.* 1865.
BURTIS, P. P., *D.* 1878.—*R. S.* 1879.—*V. P.* 1880.
BURWELL, G. N., *D.* 1846.
BURWELL, THEODOTUS, *C. S.* 1842.
BUSH, MYRON P., *D.* 1846, 1862, 1863, 1864.—*V. P.* 1847.

BUTLER, C. W., *D.* 1866.
BUTLER, J. L., *D.* 1846. – *V. P.* 1847. – *P.* 1852.
BUTLER, MORRIS. *D.* 1840.

CADY, F. L. A., *D.* 1869.
CALLENDER, S. N., *V. P.* 1836.
CAMERON, ANGUS, *D.* 1853, 1856, 1857.
CASE, HARLOW, *T.* 1839.
CHAMBERLAIN, H. S., *D.* 1836.
CHAMBERLAIN, S. M., *R. S.* 1852. – *C. S.* 1855. – *V. P.* 1856.
CLARK, SENECA A., *T.* 1879.
CLARK, THOS., *D.* 1863, 1864.
CLARKE, STEPHEN C., *D.* 1865.
CLAY, H. M., *D.* 1870.
CLEVELAND, GROVER, *D.* 1862, 1869.
CLINTON, DE WITT, *D.* 1855.
CLINTON, G. D. W., *D.* 1859.
COBB, CARLOS, *D.* 1852, 1853, 1854. – *V. P.* 1857.
COCHRANE, A. G. C., *R. S.* 1836, 1838.
COIT, GEO. JR., *D.* 1848, 1849.
COLEMAN, JNO. H., *D.* 1854.
CORNWELL, W. C., *D.* 1885, 1886, 1887.
COWING, E. H., *D.* 1850.
COWING, H. O., *D.* 1843.
COWING, JAS. A., *D.* 1839.
CRANE, THOS., *D.* 1850, 1851, 1852.
CUTTING, HARMON S., *D.* 1842, 1852.

DANFORTH, F. L., *C. S.* 1871. – *R. E. C.* 1886, 1887.
DAVIS, WM., *D.* 1846.
DAVOCK, JNO. W., *D.* 1841, *V. P.* 1842.
DAW, A. D., *R. S.* 1855. – *D.* 1856, 1860, 1861. – *V. P.* 1857, 1859, 1866.
DAWLEY, JOB S., *D.* 1872.
DAY, DAVID F., *R. S.* 1853. – *C. S.* 1856. – *D.* 1857, 1859. – *P.* 1860.
DELONG, JAS., *D.* 1839.
DEMAREST, JAS., *D.* 1855, 1856, 1862. – *C. S.* 1858.
DOBBINS, DAVID, *D.* 1860.
DOBBINS, JNO. R., *D.* 1873.
DORR. G. P., *D.* 1874.
DORSHEIMER, WM., *C. S.* 1860.
DOUGHTY, N. W., *D.* 1844, 1845.
DOYLE, PETER C., *C. S.*, 1869.
DOYLE, WM. L., *D.* 1863, 1864. – *R. S.* 1865.
DUDLEY, THOS. J. JR., *D.* 1647.
DUNBAR, G. H., *T.* 1872.
DUNBAR, J. J., *D.* 1867. – *V. P.* 1871.

EDMUNDS, THOS., *D.* 1851.
ELIAS, F. S., *D.* 1843.
EMERSON, C. I., *D.* 1842.
ENSIGN, CHAS., *D.* 1863, 1864.
EVANS, C. W., *D.* 1850. – *V. P.* 1851.

EVANS, E. T., *D.* 1864, 1870. – *V. P.* 1867. – *P.* 1868. – *R. E. C.* 1880.
EVANS, ELLICOT, *D.* 1856.
EVANS, J. C., *D.* 1838, 1839.
EVANS, L. M., *R. S.* 1866. – *D.* 1868. – *V. P.* 1871.
EWERS, TALMADGE, *D.* 1861.

FAIRCHILD, J. L., *V. P.* 1863, 1864. – *C. S.* 1866.
FARR, RINALDO, *D.* 1841. – *R. S.* 1843. – *T.* 1844, 1845, 1846.
FELTON, JNO., *D.* 1866.
FILLMORE, MILLARD, *D.* 1854.
FISH, S. H., *D.* 1853, 1854.
FISKE, CHAS., *R. S.*, 1873.
FISKE, F. W., *D.* 1858. – *V. P.* 1875.
FITCH, A. B., *D.* 1859, 1860. – *R. S.* 1862. – *V. P.* 1863, 1864.
FLAHERTY, JEREMIAH, *D.* 1843.
FLEMING, WM., *D.* 1856, 1857. – *V. P.* 1858. – *P.* 1859.
FOBES, WM. D., *D.* 1845, 1855. – *R. S.* 1846, 1847. – *V. P.* 1848, 1849.
FOLGER, E. F., *D.* 1851, 1852. – *T.* 1853, 1854.
FOLSOM, OSCAR, *C. S.* 1865. – *V. P.* 1868. – *P.* 1872.
FORD, RENSSELAER, D., *D.* 1871.
FOX, D. F., *D.* 1852.
FOX, WATSON A., *D.* 1845. – *V. P.* 1846.
FOY, ROBERT D., *D.* 1814.
FRENCH, H. C., *D.* 1876, 1883, 1884, 1885. – *R. S.* 1877.

GATES, D. F., *D.* 1863, 1864.
GARDNER, E. G., *D.* 1859.
GAYLORD, H. M., *D.* 1859.
GIBSON, JAS. C., *D.* 1848.
GLUCK, JAS. FRASER, *C.* 1885, 1886, 1887.
GOLD, CHAS. R., *D.* 1842.
GOODYEAR, C. W., *D.* 1880, 1882. – *V. P.* 1881.
GORHAM, GEO., *D.* 1881. – *V. P.* 1882, 1883. – *R. E. C.* 1884, 1885, 1886.
GRAVES, JNO. C., *D.* 1880, 1881, 1882.
GRAY, DAVID, *D.* 1862, 1869. – *C. S.* 1863, 1864. – *V. P.* 1871. – *C.* 1877, 1878.
GRAY, E. P., *D.* 1856.
GREENE, JNO. B., *D.* 1873, 1874. – *R. S.* 1875. – *V. P.* 1876. – *C.* 1877.
GREENE, WM. H., *D.* 1841, 1843.
GUENTHER, JNO. G., *D.* 1850, 1851, 1854. – *V. P.* 1852, 1855. – *P.* 1856.
GUENTHER, N. J. R., *D.* 1859.
GURNEY, WM. H., *D.* 1875. – *C. S.* 1876. – *V. P.* 1877. – *P.* 1878.
GUTHRIE, S. S., *D.* 1855.

HALBERT, N. A., *D.* 1854.
HARROUN, G. R., *D.* 1858.
HARVEY, ALEX. W., *D.* 1850, 1851, 1852. – *V. P.* 1853. – *P.* 1855.

HARVEY, C. W., *D.* 1840, 1841. — *V. P.* 1843.
HAWLEY, E. S., *D.* 1873, 1878. — *R. S.* 1874. — *C. S.* 1875, 1877. — *V. P.* 1879.
HAWLEY, ELIAS S., *R. S.* 1839, 1845. — *D.* 1840, 1841, 1847.
HAWLEY, LUCIAN, *R. S.* 1844. — *C. S.* 1852. — *V. P.* 1854.
HAWLEY, SETH C., *P.* 1836.
HAYES, EDMUND, *R. E. C.* 1887.
HAYES, GEO. B., *R. S.* 1868. — *D.* 1869, 1870, 1883, 1884, 1885.
HAYES, GEO. E., *D.* 1836. — *P.* 1838.
HAYES, JOS. L. II., *D.* 1845.
HAYWARD, GEO. W., *T.* 1866. — *D.* 1868, 1876, 1877, 1878, 1879. — *N. E. C.* 1872, 1873, 1874.
HAZARD, E. E., *V. P.* 1865, 1869.
HECOX, W. H., *V. P.* 1844, 1845.
HEFFORD, R. R., *D.* 1886.
HIBBARD, GEO. B., *D.* 1851.
HIBBARD, L. D., *D.* 1844.
HILL, J. F., *D.* 1849.
HOLLISTER, F. M., *C.* 1876, 1877, 1878, 1880, 1881, 1882, 1883, 1884.
HOLLISTER, JAS., *D.* 1840.
HOLLOWAY, ISAAC, *D.* 1859, 1870. — *V. P.* 1860, 1862, 1869.
HOLLOWAY, JNO. A., *D.* 1872, 1873.
HOLMAN, E. D., *D.* 1857.
HOLT, H. N., *D.* 1839.
HOPKINS, H. R., *D.* 1882, 1883, 1884.
HOPKINS, N. K., *D.* 1845. — *C. S.* 1846.
HOWARD, R. L., *D.* 1846, 1853, 1854, 1855, 1863, 1864, 1865. — *V. P.* 1861. — *P.* 1862.
HUBBELL, JNO., *D.* 1848. — *V. P.* 1849, 1850.
HUNT, SANFORD B., *V. P.* 1860.
HUNT, SIMON B., *D.* 1845.
HUTCHINSON, JNO. M., *D.* 1844, 1845, 1850, 1865, 1870. — *V. P.* 1846. — *P.* 1851. — *R. E. C.* 1877, 1878, 1879, 1881, 1882.

IVES, WILLIAM, *Librarian* 1852 — 1887.

JENKINS, LEWIS, *Librarian* 1850 — 1852.
JEWETT, E. R., *V. P.* 1845.
JEWETT, HENRY C., *D.* 1862, 1866.
JEWETT, JNO., *J. C. L., D.* 1865.
JEWETT, JOSIAH, *D.* 1867, 1868.
JEWETT, S. S., *P.* 1865.
JONES, H. R., *D.* 1871, 1874.
JOY, L. B., *C. S.* 1859. — *T.* 1860.
JOY, WALTER, *V. P.* 1838. — *D.* 1839. — *P.* 1840.

KEAN, THOS., *D.* 1876. — *C.* 1878, 1879, 1880, 1881, 1882, 1883.
KENNETT, THOS., *D.* 1840, 1844.
KIBBE, GEO. R., *D.* 1837, 1854.
KIMBERLY, J. L., JR., *D.* 1867.

LACY, JNO. T., *D.* 1838. - *V. P.* 1839, 1841, 1842.
LACY, W. H., *D.*, 1836.
LANGDON, G. P., *D.* 1857, 1859. — *V. P.* 1862, 1867.
LARNED, J. N., *D.* 1872, 1873. — *Superint'd't* 1877 — 1887.
LAVERACK, GEO. E., *D.* 1872, 1873, 1876, 1887. — *V. P.* 1874, 1875, 1878.
LAVERACK, WM., JR., *D.* 1838.
LAVERACK, WM. A., *D.* 1866.
LEE, JOHN R., *T.* 1836.
LEE, K. PORTER, *D.* 1874.
LENT, JAS. M., *R. S.* 1869. — *D.* 1871. — *V. P.* 1872.
LETCHWORTH, WM. P., *D.* 1858.
LEVAKE, W. S., *D.* 1842.
LEWIS, GEO. A., *R. S.* 1878. — *D.* 1879, 1880.
LOCKE, F. D., *D.* 1873. — *C. S.* 1874. — *P.* 1875.
LOCKWOOD, DANIEL N., *D.* 1870.
LOCKWOOD, JNO. F., *D.* 1852, 1853, 1854.
LOOMIS, CHAS. T., *D.* 1872, 1873, 1877. — *C. S.* 1878.
LOOMIS, THOS., *D.* 1867, 1869. — *V. P.* 1868, 1870.
LORD, T. S., *D.* 1842.
LOVERING, CHAS. F., *R. S.* 1856. — *D.* 1857.
LYON, JAS. S., *V. P.* 1870.

McCOLLUM, L. W., *R. S.* 1880. — *C. S.* 1881.
McDONALD, C. C., *D.* 1842.
McKAY, ALEX., *D.* 1839, 1845.
McMILLAN, D. H., *C. S.* 1883. — *V. P.* 1884, 1885, 1886. — *D.* 1887.
MANN, G. EDWARD, *D.* 1876.
MARSHALL, C. D., *D.* 1852. — *R. E. C.* 1887.
MARTIN, ELIJAH M., *D.* 1843.
MARTIN, H. H., *R. S.* 1858.
MATHEWS, AMOS I., *D.* 1850.
MATHEWS, GEO. B., *D.* 1881, 1883.
MERRILL, H. L., *D.* 1850.
MILBURN, JNO. G., *C.* 1879, 1880, 1881, 1882, 1884, 1885, 1886.
MILLAR, A. P., *D.* 1866.
MILLARD, H. W., *D.* 1850.
MILLER, CHAS. G., *D.* 1851, 1852. — *V. P.* 1853.
MORSE, CHAS. H., *R. S.* 1859. — *D.* 1860. — *C. S.* 1861.
MOVIUS, EDWARD, *D.* 1885, 1886. — *V. P.* 1887.
MULLIGAN, EUGENE, *D.* 1847. — *V. P.* 1848.

NEWBOULD, F. W., *D.* 1842.
NEWELL, ROBERT, *D.* 1869.
NEWHALL, DANIEL, *D.* 1876, 1879, 1880, 1881.
NEWMAN, GEO. L., *D.* 1844, 1845.
NEWMAN, JAS. M., *D.* 1841, 1843. — *R. S.* 1850. — *V. P.* 1851, 1854, 1855, 1858.
NICHOLS, A. P., *V. P.* 1843.
NIMS, OZIAS L., *D.* 1868.
NOLTON, H. G., *T.* 1850.
NORTON, CHAS. D., *C. S.* 1847. — *P.* 1850.
NORTON, CHAS. P., *D.* 1884, 1885, 1886.
NORTON, EDWARD, *P.* 1839.

NORTON, PORTER, *D.* 1887.
NOYE, R. K., *D.* 1871, 1874, 1875. — *P.* 1879.

PALMER, EVERARD, *D.* 1853, 1861, 1865. — *C. S.* 1854. —
  V. P. 1855, 1856. — *P.* 1857.
PALMER, HARLOW, *D.* 1845, 1846, 1847.
PEABODY, W. H., *D.* 1860, 1861.
PEASE, JNO., JR., *D.* 1867.
PENFIELD, JAS. H., *D.* 1860, 1861.
PETERS, T. C., *D.* 1838. — *V. P.* 1839.
PICKERING, E. P., *T.* 1847.
PLIMPTON, GEO. D., *T.* 1869.
PLUMB, RALPH H., *D.* 1885, 1886. — *V. P.* 1887.
POOLE, R., *D.* 1836.
POOLEY, CHAS. A., *D.* 1887.
POWERS, JNO., *D.* 1857.
PRATT, P. P., *D.* 1843.
PRATT, S. F., *D.* 1838, 1839, 1840.
PUTNAM, GEO. P., *C. S.* 1870.
PUTNAM, JAS. O., *D.* 1846.
PUTNAM, JNO. S., *D.* 1842.

RAMSDELL, THOS. S., *D.* 1875, 1876, 1880, 1881. — *C. S.* 1879.
RAYMOND, CHAS. H., *D.* 1836, 1838, 1839, 1840, 1841.
RAYNOR, AUG., *D.* 1838.
RICH, ED. S., *T.* 1861, 1862, 1863, 1864.
RICH, G. BARRETT, *T.* 1871. — *V. P.* 1873, 1874, 1875. — *D.* 1877.
RICHMOND, ALONZO, *D.* 1873.
RICHMOND, HENRY A., *D.* 1862, 1863, 1865. — *V. P.* 1864. — *P.* 1869.
RICHMOND, JEWETT M., *D.* 1884. — *P.* 1885, 1886, 1887.
ROCHESTER, JAS. H., *T.* 1842.
ROCHESTER, NATHANIEL, *D.* 1878, 1879, 1882, 1883. —
  C. S. 1880. — *R. S.* 1881.
ROCHESTER, WM. B., *D.* 1852.
ROGERS, PERRY, P. *R. S.* 1854. — *D.* 1855.
ROGERS, SHERMAN S., *D.* 1862.
ROLLINS, A., *D.* 1843.
ROOT, A. R., *D.* 1858, 1859.
ROUNDS, E. H., *R. S.* 1884, 1885, 1886. — *D.* 1887.
ROUNDS, GEO. W., *D.* 1852.
RUMRILL, H., *D.* 1846.
RUMSEY, B. C., *D.* 1849, 1862. — *T.* 1850, 1851, 1852. —
  P. 1853.
RUMSEY, D. P., *V. P.* 1865, 1867.
RUSSELL, ROBERT, *R. S.* 1857.
RUSSELL, WING., *D.* 1838.

SAGE, H. H., *D.* 1855, 1856.
SALISBURY, GUY H., *D.* 1842, 1843. — *R. S.* 1848. —
  C. S. 1849. — *V. P.* 1850.
SARGEANT, PHINEAS, *Librarian* 1839 — 1850.
SAWYER, JAS. D., *D.* 1853, 1854, 1855, 1858.
SEARS, F. A., *D.* 1856, 1861. — *T.* 1858. — *V. P.* 1860.

SEYMOUR, H. S., *D.* 1841.
SHATTUCK, CHAS. T., *D.* 1844.
SHELDON, JAS., *D.* 1844, 1845. — *V. P.* 1846. — *P.* 1848.
SHERMAN, ISAAC, *D.* 1846, 1849.
SHERWOOD, ALBERT, *P.* 1866.
SHIELS, THOS., *D.* 1858.
SICARD, GEO. J., *C.* 1883, 1884, 1885.
SIDWAY, FRANK, *D.* 1865.
SIMONS, SEWARD A., *D.* 1885, 1886, 1887.
SIMPSON, C. D., *D.* 1875.
SIRRET, WM. B., *D.* 1871, 1872. — *V. P.* 1873.
SIZER, THOS. J., *R. S.* 1840, 1841, 1842.
SMITH, EDWARD B., *D.* 1865, 1866. — *P.* 1883, 1884. —
  R. E. C. 1885, 1886.
SMITH, EDWIN, *T.* 1843.
SMITH, H. K., *D.* 1836.
SMITH, JAS. M., *C. S.* 1843. — *V. P.* 1844. — *R. E. C.* 1872.
SMITH, JUNIUS S., *D.* 1861.
SMITH, WM. L. G., *C. S.* 1840. — *P.* 1842.
SNOW, FRANK M., *D.* 1856. — *T.* 1857. — *V. P.* 1858, 1859.
SPENCER, RAY T., *R. S.* 1871. — *D.* 1872, 1873.
SPRAGUE, E. CARLTON, *D.* 1847. — *V. P.* 1849, 1852. —
  P. 1876.
SPRAGUE, HENRY S., *D.* 1877, 1879, 1880, 1881, 1883. —
  V. P. 1878, 1882. — *C. S.* 1884.
SPRAGUE, HENRY WARE, *D.* 1886, 1887.
STARR, GEO. W., *D.* 1850.
STEELE, O. G., *D.* 1836. — *V. P.* 1838. — *R. E. C.* 1872, 1873, 1874, 1875, 1876.
STEELE, O. G., JR., *D.* 1867, 1868.
STERLING, A. S., *D.* 1842, 1844.
STEVENS, EDWARD, *V. P.* 1861.
STEVENS, MILO, *D.* 1858.
STEVENS, F. P., *C. S.* 1836.
STEVENSON, E. L., *R. E. C.* 1876, 1877, 1878, 1879, 1880, 1881.
STOCKING, THOS. R., *D.* 1838. — *V. P.* 1839, 1840.
STORRS, O. S., *R. S.* 1872. — *V. P.* 1873.
STRINGHAM, H. T., *T.* 1848, 1849.
SWAN, E. A., *D.* 1857.
SWEENEY, JAS., *D.* 1867.
SWEET, CHAS. A., *D.* 1871. — *V. P.* 1872, 1874. — *P.* 1881. — *R. E. C.* 1882, 1883, 1884.
SWEET, WM. C., *D.* 1858. — *T.* 1859. — *V. P.* 1861, 1862.

TABER, WM. D., *D.* 1847. — *V. P.* 1848.
TAYLOR, MARTIN, *D.* 1868, 1870, 1872.
TELLER, GEO. R., *D.* 1881, 1882, 1883.
THOMPSON, WM. A., *V. P.* 1841.
TOWNSEND, E. CORNING, *D.* 1887.
TOWNSEND, GEO. W., *R. S.* 1860. — *D.* 1866.
TREAT, WM., *R. S.* 1849.
TROWBRIDGE, J. S., *D.* 1849.
TRUSCOTT, GEO., *P.* 1867.

UTLEY, HORACE, *D.* 1849.

VAN DEVENTER, J. T., *D.* 1855. — *V. P.* 1856.
VIELE, H. K., *C. S.* 1839. — *V. P.* 1840, 1841.
VIELE, SHELDON T., *C.* 1886, 1887.
VOUGHT, JNO. H., *V. P.* 1868.

WADSWORTH, CHAS. F., *V. P.* 1865, 1866. — *P.* 1870.
WADSWORTH, JAS., *D.* 1853.
WALBRIDGE, C. E., *D.* 1874, 1875.
WALBRIDGE, GEO. B., *D.* 1838.
WALBRIDGE, WELLS D., *D.* 1847, 1849. — *C. S.* 1848. — *V. P.* 1850, 1851, 1852, 1853. — *P.* 1854.
WALKER, JESSE, *C. S.* 1838.
WALKER, WM. H., *D.* 1849. — *V. P.* 1862.
WARD, WM. R. L., *D.* 1842.
WARDWELL, GEO. S., *D.* 1860, 1861, 1868. — *V. P.* 1869. — *P.* 1871. — *R. E. C.* 1873, 1874, 1875.
WARDWELL, WM. T., *D.* 1853, 1857, 1862. — *T.* 1854, 1856. — *P.* 1858.
WARREN, JOS., *D.* 1858, 1864. — *P.* 1861.
WARREN, O. G., *C. S.* 1873. — *D.* 1874, 1875, 1877, 1878. — *V. P.* 1876, 1879.
WASHBURN, MARCELLINUS, *D.* 1860.
WATSON, H. M., *D.* 1884, 1885, 1886.
WATSON, S. V. R., *P.* 1863, 1864.
WEBSTER, GEO. C., *D.* 1847.

WELCH, SAMUEL M., *D.* 1869.
WELCH, SAMUEL M., JR., *D.* 1872, 1876, 1878, 1879. — *V. P.* 1880.
WELCH, THOS. C., *C. S.* 1843, 1845. — *P.* 1847.
WHEELER, CHAS. B., *C. S.* 1882, 1886, 1887. — *V. P.* 1883, 1884. — *D.* 1885.
WHITE, H. G., *D.* 1848.
WHITE, WM. L., *D.* 1874, 1875.
WILCOX, CHAS. H., *D.* 1846, 1849.
WILKESON, SAMUEL, JR., *V. P.* 1842.
WILLIAMS, CHAS. H., *D.* 1866.
WILLIAMS, F. F., *R. S.* 1887.
WILLIAMS, GEO. L., *D.* 1876, 1877.
WILLIAMS, GIBSON T., *V. P.* 1844, 1845. — *D.* 1863, 1864.
WILLIAMS, H. R., *D.* 1836.
WILLIAMS, JNO. L., *R. S.* 1867. — *D.* 1870, 1875. — *T.* 1876, 1878, 1880, 1881, 1882, 1883, 1884, 1885, 1886, 1887.
WILSON, ROBERT P., *D.* 1871, 1874, 1875. — *V. P.* 1872. — *P.* 1877. — *R. E. C.* 1878, 1879, 1880, 1881, 1882, 1883.
WING, H. R., *D.* 1836.
WINNE, CHAS., *V. P.* 1836.
WOODRUFF, L. C., *D.* 1869.
WRIGHT, A. J., *R. S.* 1882. — *D.* 1883, 1884.
WRIGHT, THOS. H., *D.* 1844.

YOUNG, CHAS. E., *V. P.* 1859. — *D.* 1861.

++++++++++++++++++++++++++++++++

THE LIBRARY SERVICE, 1887.

Superintendent,   J. N. LARNED.
Librarian,   WILLIAM IVES.

ASSISTANTS.

Cataloguing,	EVA M. JUDD.
Book Delivery,	Mrs. H. B. RANSOM, HELEN I. CLARK, FANNY B. MEISTER, CHARLES H. STAUCH.
Periodicals,	FLORENCE A. MOON.
Ladies' Reading Room,	Mrs. MARGARET L. LARK.
Sunday Service,	EMILIE BOVET, FANNY B. MEISTER.
Janitor and Engineer,	JOHN KRIEG.
Janitress,	Mrs. JOHN KRIEG.

www.ingramcontent.com/pod-product-compliance
Lightning Source LLC
Chambersburg PA
CBHW031606110426
42742CB00037B/1308